Wonders of the World

The Great Barrier Reef

Erinn Banting

MEDIA ENHANCED BOOKS
AV2 BY WEIGL
ADDED VALUE · AUDIO VISUAL

www.av2books.com

MEDIA ENHANCED BOOKS
AV²
BY WEIGL™
ADDED VALUE • AUDIO VISUAL

AV² provides enriched content that supplements and complements this book. Weigl's AV² books strive to create inspired learning and engage young minds in a total learning experience.

Your AV² Media Enhanced books come alive with...

Audio
Listen to sections of the book read aloud.

Key Words
Study vocabulary, and complete a matching word activity.

Video
Watch informative video clips.

Quizzes
Test your knowledge.

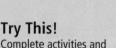
Embedded Weblinks
Gain additional information for research.

Slide Show
View images and captions, and prepare a presentation.

Go to **www.av2books.com**, and enter this book's unique code.

BOOK CODE

J551826

Try This!
Complete activities and hands-on experiments.

... and much, much more!

AV² **by Weigl** brings you media enhanced books that support active learning.

Published by AV² by Weigl
350 5th Avenue, 59th Floor
New York, NY 10118
Website: www.av2books.com   www.weigl.com

Library of Congress Cataloging-in-Publication Data available upon request
ISBN 978-1-61913-525-3 (hard cover)
ISBN 978-1-61913-438-6 (soft cover)

Printed in the United States of America in North Mankato, Minnesota
1 2 3 4 5 6 7 8 9   16 15 14 13 12

062012
WEP170512

Editor Aaron Carr
Design Mandy Christiansen

Every reasonable effort has been made to trace ownership and to obtain permission to reprint copyright material. The publishers would be pleased to have any errors or omissions brought to their attention so that they may be corrected in subsequent printings.

Photo Credits
Weigl acknowledges Getty Images as its primary photo supplier for this title.

Contents

The Wonder Down Under

T he spectacular Great Barrier Reef is the largest coral reef in the world. It is located off the coast of Australia, one of the most southerly continents on Earth. Australia is so far south of the equator that people call it "down under."

The Great Barrier Reef is not only beautiful, it is also an important **ecosystem**. Scientists study the reef to learn how its many animals live and interact with their environment. Fishers rely on the reef to provide fish for them to catch in nearby waters. Tourists visit the reef to scuba dive and learn about nature.

The Great Barrier Reef stretches more than 1,600 miles (2,600 kilometers).

Six species of sea turtles come to Great Barrier Reef to breed.

Great Barrier Reef Facts

- The Great Barrier Reef stretches about 1,250 miles (2,012 km) along Australia's northeast coast.

- The Great Barrier Reef is the largest structure in the world that was built by living organisms.

- There are more than 10,000 different **species** of animals living in the Great Barrier Reef. Some have never been named by scientists.

- The Great Barrier Reef is considered one of the Seven Wonders of the Natural World. This is a list of the most amazing natural sites in the world.

- In 1975, the Australian government established the Great Barrier Reef Marine Park to protect the coral reef and its surrounding waters. This huge park covers about 134,000 square miles (347,058 sq. km).

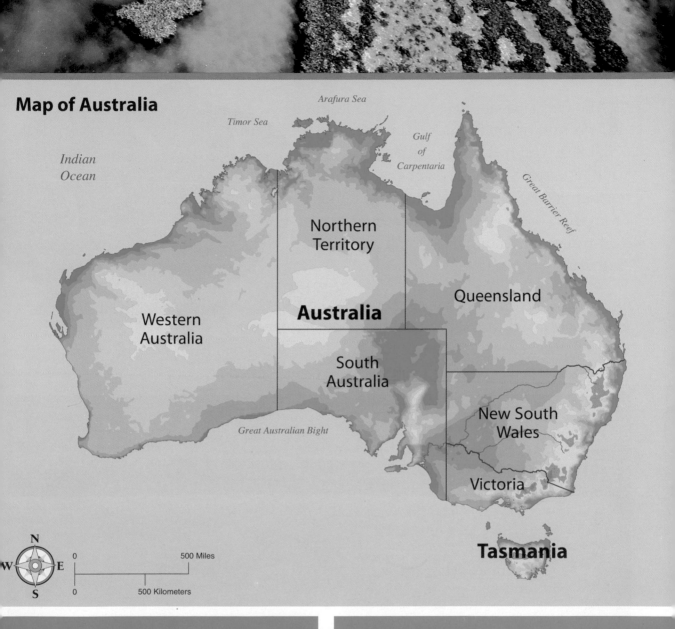

Map of Australia

Arafura Sea

Timor Sea

Gulf
of
Carpentaria

*Indian
Ocean*

Great Barrier Reef

Northern
Territory

Queensland

Australia

Western
Australia

South
Australia

New South
Wales

Great Australian Bight

Victoria

N
W E
S

0   500 Miles

0   500 Kilometers

Tasmania

The Great Barrier Reef is made up of more than 400 types of coral.

About 630 species of echinoderm live on the Great Barrier Reef, including starfish.

Where in the World?

The Great Barrier Reef lies in a southern portion of the Pacific Ocean called the Coral Sea. The reef begins in the Torres Strait, a narrow body of water that separates northern Australia from Papua New Guinea. From the Torres Strait, the Great Barrier Reef runs south along nearly half of Australia's eastern coast.

The clownfish is one of the more than 1,500 species of fish that lives on the reef.

On a map, the Great Barrier Reef looks like a long, underwater wall that separates Australia from the sea. The reef, however, is not a solid wall. It is made up of about 3,000 small reefs and coral islands called cays.

The wonders of the reef lie very close to the water's surface.

Puzzler

The Great Barrier Reef is located in the Pacific Ocean. This is one of the major oceans of the world.

Q: Can you name some of the major oceans of the world?

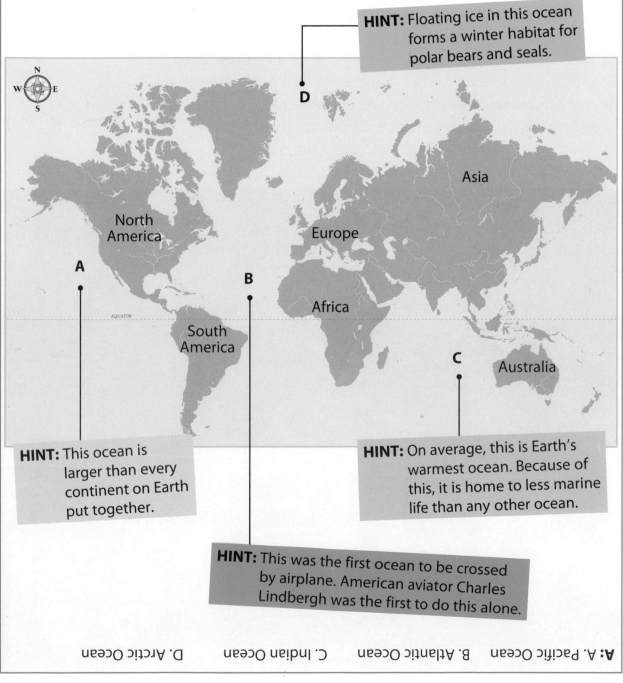

HINT: Floating ice in this ocean forms a winter habitat for polar bears and seals.

D

Asia

North America

Europe

A

B

Africa

EQUATOR

South America

C

Australia

HINT: This ocean is larger than every continent on Earth put together.

HINT: On average, this is Earth's warmest ocean. Because of this, it is home to less marine life than any other ocean.

HINT: This was the first ocean to be crossed by airplane. American aviator Charles Lindbergh was the first to do this alone.

A: A. Pacific Ocean   B. Atlantic Ocean   C. Indian Ocean   D. Arctic Ocean

A Trip Back in Time

The sea floor on which the Great Barrier Reef sits was formed about 500,000 years ago. Today's reef, however, is very different in size and shape. Coral lives on top of many layers of dead coral from centuries ago.

Coral **polyps** start the process of reef building. These tiny creatures attach themselves to coral rock or other hard surfaces underwater. Polyps become coral as they grow hard skeletons outside their bodies. When certain kinds of coral die, their skeleton shell remains. A reef consists of many of these dead, rocky corals connected to each other. As new polyps grow on dead coral, the life cycle starts over.

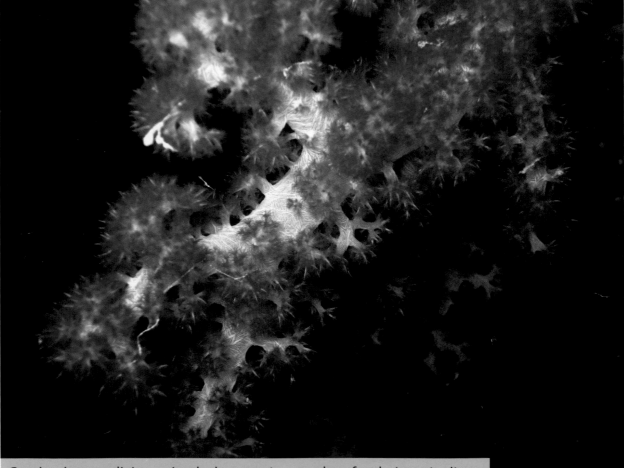

Coral polyps are living animals that stay in one place for their entire lives.

Different Kinds of Reefs

Not all coral reefs grow in the same way. The chart below shows the three main kinds of reefs. The orange areas represent coral reef.

SIDE VIEW	OVERHEAD VIEW	TYPE
		Fringe reefs grow in very shallow water surrounding land, such as coasts or islands. These are the youngest types of reefs.
		Barrier reefs grow in deeper water a bit farther offshore. They form a wall, or barrier, between the sea and the shore. A lagoon sits between the reef and shore.
		Atolls are ringed reefs that form away from shore. Some atolls grow around the rim of a sunken volcano.

The Coral Reef Ecosystem

Living communities in nature are called ecosystems. Animals, plants, and the surrounding environment all contribute to making an ecosystem work. Members of ecosystems are divided into groups called producers, consumers, and decomposers. Each of these groups depends on the others for survival.

In the Great Barrier Reef, producers are creatures, such as **algae**, that are eaten by consumers. Coral polyps are consumers that feed off the algae that grow nearby. Thousands of types of fish are also coral reef consumers.

Decomposers, such as **bacteria**, are creatures that clean the reef. They eat the waste materials that other animals and plants leave behind.

The sea cucumber is not a vegetable. It is an animal and a decomposer. It crawls along the reef floor, eating waste material.

Coral Threat

The crown-of-thorns starfish is a dangerous member of the Great Barrier Reef community. Since 1965, scientists have observed periods when the crown-of-thorns population suddenly increased in the reef. This type of starfish is a **predator** of coral. It feeds directly on live coral polyps. So, when the crown-of-thorns population increases, it kills off far too much coral and threatens the entire reef ecosystem.

It is difficult for humans to remove the crown-of-thorns starfish from the reef. This dangerous creature is covered with poisonous spines.

Life in the Reef

Some of the most unique and beautiful creatures in the world live in the Great Barrier Reef. Clown, parrot, mandarin, and thousands of other types of fish dart through the coral looking for food and shelter.

Larger animals, such as sharks and whales, live nearby. Crabs and sea turtles live in the reef waters, but they sometimes leave the water and crawl around on the beaches.

Many Great Barrier Reef beaches are home to hundreds of bird species, including sandpipers, herons, and terns. These birds are also part of the coral reef ecosystem, as they eat fish from the water. Many birds are just visitors to the area. They **migrate** to Australia every winter from colder countries in the north.

The blue-ringed octopus is one of the reef's deadliest creatures. If bitten by this octopus, an adult human could die in just a few minutes.

Coral Character

About 400 different species of coral live in the Great Barrier Reef. They take on many different shapes and colors. Only stony corals grow skeletons outside their bodies and become reefs when they die. Other corals, such as gorgonian coral, grow spines inside their bodies. They do not turn into coral reefs.

The color of coral comes from the algae they eat. Only living corals have color. Dead coral turns white. Coral "bleaching" is a term scientists use when large amounts of coral die and turn white. Bleaching is usually caused by a drastic change in the reef environment. In 1998, sea temperatures around the world increased suddenly, and coral bleaching destroyed large parts of reefs in Australia and other parts of the world.

A certain species of stony coral is called "brain coral."

Early Explorers

The first people to discover the Great Barrier Reef were the **Aboriginal Australians**, who arrived in Australia about 50,000 years ago.

Aboriginal groups lived mostly on the coast of Australia and islands of the reef. Explorers from Asia and Europe visited Australia's shores between the 1300s and 1700s. These visitors did not settle in Australia because the land was hard to farm and was far away from their home countries. When English explorer James Cook sailed to Australia in 1770, he claimed the land for England.

When Captain James Cook arrived in Australia, he named it New South Wales. It reminded him of a part of Great Britain called Wales.

Biography

Matthew Flinders (1774–1814)

In 1802, the well-known British sea explorer Matthew Flinders set sail from England on a very important journey. Flinders was the first person to sail around the entire Australian continent and carefully map its shores. The Great Barrier Reef posed a challenge to ship captains. The sharp, rocky reefs could rip the bottom out of a wooden ship. After several attempts, Flinders succeeded in finding a safe passage through the reef. He spent two years exploring Australia. Today, this path is called Flinders Passage.

In 1814, Flinders' journals about this journey were published as a book titled *A Voyage to Terra Australis*. Flinders died at the age of 40 on the same day that his book was published.

Facts of Life

Born: 1774

Hometown: Donington, England

Occupation: Explorer, navigator

Died: 1814

The Big Picture

Coral reefs exist in many places around the world. They need shallow, warm water to support their complex ecosystem. This map shows some of the major coral reefs and the bodies of water that are their homes.

Florida Keys
Atlantic Ocean

NORTH AMERICA

ATLANTIC OCEAN

Mexico
Caribbean Sea

EQUATOR

PACIFIC OCEAN

SOUTH AMERICA

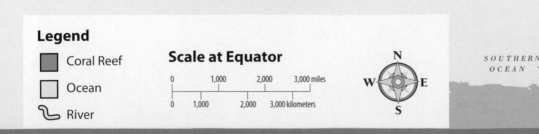

Legend

- Coral Reef
- Ocean
- River

Scale at Equator

0   1,000   2,000   3,000 miles

0   1,000   2,000   3,000 kilometers

N
W   E
S

SOUTHERN OCEAN

Red Sea Riviera Reefs
Red Sea

Philippine Islands
Pacific Ocean

Indian Ocean Coral Reef
Indian Ocean

The Great Barrier Reef
Pacific Ocean

ARCTIC OCEAN

ASIA

EUROPE

PACIFIC
OCEAN

AFRICA

INDIAN
OCEAN

AUSTRALIA

SOUTHERN
OCEAN

ANTARCTICA

People of the Reef

Aboriginal Australians and Torres Strait Islanders had lived in Australia for thousands of years before European explorers arrived. Aboriginal Australians lived in areas near the Great Barrier Reef, and Torres Strait Islanders lived on northern islands between Australia and Papua New Guinea. When Europeans began building colonies in Australia, many of these **indigenous** peoples were treated poorly, sometimes violently. As newcomers built more cities and towns, indigenous peoples were forced out of places where they had lived for generations. Eventually, Aboriginal Australians were forced to live in Australia's hot, dry, inland region called the Outback.

Today, indigenous Australian people have reclaimed some of their homelands. They are treated with more respect by the Australian government. Indigenous peoples are involved in decisions about managing the reef environment.

One of Australia's main landmarks is Uluru, which stands on Aboriginal land.

Dugongs

Aboriginal Australians and Torres Strait Islanders believe nature is **sacred**. For instance, sea mammals called dugongs are very special creatures in these peoples' cultures. Dugongs are worshiped, but they are also hunted for food.

The dugong is an **endangered** species. Overhunting could cause it to become extinct. The Australian government allows Aboriginal Australians to hunt a controlled number of dugongs. In return, the Aboriginal people work to protect the animals and ensure they will remain a part of the Great Barrier Reef forever.

Dugongs live off the Australian coast and in other areas of the Pacific and Indian Oceans.

5–4 billion years ago
Earth forms.

600–300 million years ago
Seas rise and fall over each of Earth's continents.

65 million years ago
Dinosaurs become extinct.

50 million years ago
Australia separates from the other continents.

500,000 years ago
Land forms where the Great Barrier Reef now sits.

50,000 years ago
Aboriginal Australians are living in Australia.

10,000 years ago
The **Ice Age** ends, and water levels rise.

8,000–6,000 years ago
The Great Barrier Reef begins to form.

1400s
Chinese explorer Zheng He (1371–1433) explores Australia's north coast.

1642–1644
Dutch explorer Abel Tasman (1603–1659) visits and maps parts of Australia.

1770
James Cook claims Australia for England.

1788
England officially establishes the colony of New South Wales in Australia.

1643 Abel Tasman completes a 10-week trip around the continent of Australia.

50,000 years ago Aboriginal Australians and Torres Straight Islanders are the first inhabitants of the Great Barrier Reef area.

1901 The Duke and Duchess of Cornwall and York visit Melbourne to open the First Commonwealth Parliament of Australia.

1975 The Great Barrier Reef Marine Park is established to protect large parts of the reef.

2002 The Great Barrier Reef suffers its most devasting mass coral bleaching on record.

Present People can tour the Great Barrier Reef in semi-submarines.

1801–1803
Matthew Flinders explores and maps the Australian coast.

1901
Australia becomes a **commonwealth**.

1930s
The first hotel resorts are built on the Great Barrier Reef coast and islands.

1960s
Scientists become aware of crown-of-thorns starfish outbreaks, which damage large areas of coral.

1975
The Australian government establishes the Great Barrier Reef Marine Park to protect the reef and surrounding area.

1981
The United Nations Educational, Scientific and Cultural Organization (UNESCO) names the Great Barrier Reef as a World Heritage Site.

1998
Warming sea temperatures cause massive coral bleaching in many worldwide coral reefs, including the Great Barrier Reef.

2002
Almost 60 percent of the Great Barrier Reef suffers from coral bleaching as temperatures continue to rise.

2009
The Great Barrier Reef Marine Park Authority releases a report outlining the biggest threats to the Great Barrier Reef, including rising temperatures, higher sea levels, and **acidification**.

Protecting the Reef

The Great Barrier Reef is one of the healthiest coral reefs in the world, but it must be protected to survive. Many of Australia's 19 million people live in or near coastline cities. Large numbers of people living and building cities in these areas create threats to the reef. Industries, such as construction, fishing, logging, and manufacturing, can add **pollution** to the air and water. Pollution can disrupt or destroy the coral reef ecosystem.

Individual people also can cause damage. Fishers who drop boat anchors sometimes break off large pieces of coral. Scuba divers can harm certain sea creatures simply by touching them. Even the activity of swimming can cause problems. Scientists believe that human sweat and suntan lotion that washes off swimmers can disrupt the chemical balance in reef waters.

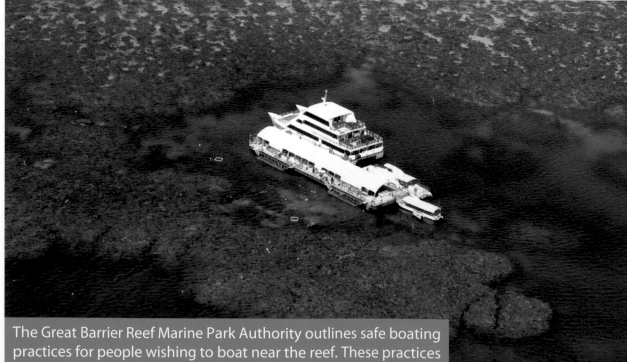

The Great Barrier Reef Marine Park Authority outlines safe boating practices for people wishing to boat near the reef. These practices are aimed at reducing potential harmful effects of boating.

The Australian government has passed laws limiting the areas where people can fish and dive. Much of the reef is a protected national park, so damaging the reef is illegal. The growth of human communities, however, is more difficult to control. What can the government do to stop towns and cities from expanding in one of the most beautiful spots on Earth?

Should the government restrict human activity on the Great Barrier Reef?

Yes	No
Industries can cause pollution in Great Barrier Reef waters.	The Australian coast is beautiful, and people want to experience the reef.
Fishing interferes with the ecosystem by taking certain animals out of the reef.	Fishing these waters brings a large amount of money into the economy.
Scuba divers and other swimmers can disturb the ecosystem.	If people can scuba dive in the reef, they may become aware of its importance. They will be more likely to preserve the area.

Natural Attractions

There are many things to see and do on a trip to the Great Barrier Reef. People from around the world visit this area to enjoy its natural beauty. Snorkeling and scuba diving are popular activities in the reef. People wear masks and special gear so they can spend a great deal of time underwater. Divers are advised to look at the underwater life but not to touch. Many of the sea creatures are beautiful, but some can be dangerous to humans.

Visitors also love to fish in the reef area, but strict rules govern where and how people may fish. The Australian government makes every effort to ensure that human visitors do not damage the precious reef.

Divers must be careful not to interfere with the reef ecosystem. Simply breaking off a piece of coral can destroy hundreds of years of growth.

Recipe

In Australia, the weather is almost always warm, so people eat outdoors on "barbies," or barbecues. Even restaurants serve food cooked on barbies, including vegetables, meat, fresh fish, and freshly caught seafood. Ask an adult to help you make this delicious Australian dish.

Australian Shrimp on the Barbie (serves 8)

1–2 cups (118 milliliters) melted butter

1–4 cups (59 ml) olive oil

mixed herbs (1 teaspoon each of thyme, parsley, and cilantro)

3 tablespoons fresh lemon juice

3 crushed garlic cloves

1 tablespoon chopped shallot

1–2 pounds (680 grams) peeled shrimp

salt and pepper to taste

lemon wedges

1. Clean and peel the shrimp. Combine the butter, oil, herbs, lemon juice, garlic, and shallots in a large bowl. Mix in the shrimp and let sit in the refrigerator for 1 hour.

2. Place the shrimp on skewers, and grill on medium heat until they are pink on both sides (about 2 minutes). Serve with lemon wedges.

Stories from the Reef

The earliest stories told in Australia were Aboriginal tales of "The Dreaming" or "Dreamtime." The Dreaming explains many Aboriginal religious beliefs, such as how the world began. To this day, indigenous peoples tell and act out stories about the places in Australia they consider sacred, including the Great Barrier Reef.

When early English explorers visited Australia, they wrote adventure stories about the treacherous conditions in the country and the oceans surrounding it. Legends about terrifying sea creatures inspired French author Jules Verne to write *20,000 Leagues Under the Sea* in 1870. It is a thrilling novel that takes place partly in Australia.

The reef continues to enchant people today. In 2003, the animated film *Finding Nemo* brought the Great Barrier Reef to life on movie screens around the world.

This ancient rock painting tells part of an Aboriginal Dreamtime story about fabled sea creatures.

Music in Nature

Aboriginal Australians invented some of the world's most unique musical instruments. One of the best-known Australian instruments is the didgeridoo. Originally, these long, hollow instruments were made from tree branches that had been hollowed out by termites. Today, most are made with tools by craftspeople.

The low sounds made when musicians blow through a didgeridoo imitate sounds in nature, such as running water, swaying trees, and thunder. Even some of Australia's pop and rock music groups use didgeridoo music.

Didgeridoos are beautifully decorated for Aboriginal ceremonies.

True or False?

Decide whether the following statements are true or false.
If the statement is false, make it true.

1. About 1,000 species of animals live in the Great Barrier Reef.

2. The Great Barrier Reef is made up of many different reefs and coral islands, or cays.

3. Matthew Flinders was the first person to sail around Australia and map its shores.

4. Captain James Cook brought the first people to inhabit Australia.

5. Coral is not alive.

6. The dugong is an endangered animal of the coral reef.

ANSWERS

1. False. About 10,000 species live in the Great Barrier Reef.
2. True
3. True
4. False. Aboriginal Australians and Torres Strait Islanders had been living there for thousands of years.
5. False. Coral is a living animal, but some kinds of corals turn to rock-like structures after they die.
6. True

Short Answer

Answer the following questions using information from the book.

1. How many kinds of coral reef are there?
2. Who wrote *20,000 Leagues Under the Sea*?
3. How long have Aboriginal Australians lived in Australia?
4. What are the names of the world's major oceans?
5. How does building construction threaten a coral reef?

Multiple Choice

Choose the best answer for the following questions.

1. Aboriginal Australians make didgeridoos from:
    a. paper
    b. tree branches
    c. coral

2. What animal can damage the coral reef?
    a. crown-of-thorns starfish
    b. soft coral
    c. whales

3. What are newly formed corals called?
    a. baby coral
    b. coral pups
    c. polyps

4. What happens during coral bleaching?
    a. coral dies
    b. coral is washed
    c. coral is born

Activity

Acid in the Oceans

Human activity has a major impact on the world's oceans. Vehicles and power plants produce a gas known as carbon dioxide, which dissolves into the ocean. Carbon dioxide makes the water more acidic. Acidic water makes the shells of animals such as corals and crabs thinner and easier to break. Try this experiment to see how these creatures might be affected by acidic ocean water.

Materials

2 Large Glasses

Vinegar

Water

Teaspoon

Baking Soda

Instructions

1 Fill each glass with water.

2 Stir two teaspoons of baking soda into each glass, and let it settle to the bottom.

3 Add one teaspoon of vinegar to one glass, and stir. Watch what happens to the baking soda.

Results

You probably saw the baking soda dissolve when you added the vinegar. Baking soda is made up of a similar substance to the shells of sea creatures such as corals, clams, and crabs. The more acidic the water, the more easily shells dissolve. For this reason, reducing carbon dioxide pollution is a major step in saving coral reefs around the world.

Key Words

Aboriginal Australians: the first peoples to live in Australia

acidification: the process of being converted into an acid

algae: simple living things; tiny plant life that has no roots or flowers

bacteria: tiny living cells that cannot be seen without a microscope

commonwealth: a country or state governed by the people who live there, rather than by a king or queen

ecosystem: a group of living plants, animals, and their environment, all of which act as a community

endangered: threatened; nearly extinct

Ice Age: a period in Earth's history when huge glaciers covered large parts of the planet

indigenous: native to a certain place; having been born in a place

migrate: to move from one place to another

pollution: materials that can harm the air, water, or land

polyps: small, tube-shaped sea creatures with tentacles for catching food

predator: an animal that hunts and kills other animals for food

sacred: spiritual, religious, and holy

species: a specific group of plant or animal that shares characteristics

Index

Log on to www.av2books.com

AV² by Weigl brings you media enhanced books that support active learning. Go to www.av2books.com, and enter the special code found on page 2 of this book. You will gain access to enriched and enhanced content that supplements and complements this book. Content includes video, audio, weblinks, quizzes, a slide show, and activities.

Audio
Listen to sections of the book read aloud.

Video
Watch informative video clips.

Embedded Weblinks
Gain additional information for research.

Try This!
Complete activities and hands-on experiments.

WHAT'S ONLINE?

Try This!	Embedded Weblinks	Video	EXTRA FEATURES
Map where the Great Barrier Reef is and the features that surround it.	Learn more about the Great Barrier Reef.	Take a flight over the Great Barrier Reef.	**Audio** Listen to sections of the book read aloud.
Write a biography of an explorer of the Great Barrier Reef region.	Play games related to the Great Barrier Reef.	Watch a video about the issues facing the Great Barrier Reef.	**Key Words** Study vocabulary, and complete a matching word activity.
Locate major coral reefs around the world.	Find out more about early explorers of the Great Barrier Reef.		
Complete a timeline that outlines the history of the Great Barrier Reef.			**Slide Show** View images and caption and prepare a presentatio
Test your knowledge of the Great Barrier Reef.			**Quizzes** Test your knowledge.

AV² was built to bridge the gap between print and digital. We encourage you to tell us what you like and what you want to see in the future.
Sign up to be an AV² Ambassador at www.av2books.com/ambassador.

Due to the dynamic nature of the Internet, some of the URLs and activities provided as part of AV² by Weigl may have changed or ceased to exist. AV² by Weigl accepts no responsibility for any such changes. All media enhanced books are regularly monitored to update addresses and sites in a timely manner. Contact AV² by Weigl at 1-866-649-3445 or av2books@weigl.com with any questions, comments, or feedback.